WHY WORKING-FROM-ANYWHERE-COMPANIES ATTRACT THE BEST TALENT

A GUIDE FOR COMPANIES, EMPLOYEES AND REMOTE JOB SEEKERS

MARTIN JACOBS

Copyright © 2019 by Martin Jacobs

All rights reserved.

No part of this book may be reproduced in any form or by any electronic or mechanical means, including information storage and retrieval systems, without written permission from the author, except for the use of brief quotations in a book review.

Formatted by Kristen Forbes (deviancepress.com)

CONTENTS

Introduction   v

1. How to Know If Remote Work is Right for You   1
2. Exploring Different Types of Remote Work   13
3. 6 Common Myths About Telecommuting   21
4. Remote Work and the Bottom Line   27
5. How to Convert a Position to Remote Only   35
6. 6 Ways to Promote Inclusivity with Remote Workers   41
7. 5 Strategies for Networking When You Work Remotely   49
8. 6 Perks of Working From Home   57
9. How Working Remotely Affects Productivity   65
10. Community & Global Effects of Remote Work   71
11. 5 Necessary Skills for Current or Aspiring Remote Workers   79
12. Resources for Remote Workers   87
13. Resources for Employers of Aspiring & Current Remote Workers   95
14. Future Directions for Remote Work   103

INTRODUCTION

WORKING REMOTELY

The thought of working remotely from a home office, or from somewhere else, has always brought with it some anxiety. How can you make sure your company knows you are working as hard as if you were at the office? How do you meet as frequently with different groups of people and build up networks? How can you be the go-to person for your employees when you are not physically there? Part of my paranoia was certainly driven by my own stereotypes of remote workers lounging in a hammock in PJ's and napping between every other email.

I tried different measures to make myself more comfortable when trying to work remotely. I got up extra early and stayed up extra late to ensure I answered all emails immediately and maintained a visible online presence. For a while, I decided to wear a tie and suit at my home office. On her way out to work, my wife told me to just relax a little. I made more than the necessary amount of calls just to catch up with my boss, peers and fellow employees. And the list goes on.

All these changes helped a little bit, but did not satisfy my desire to make a case for working from home – not for me, and not for others. Going back to the office, having that face-to-face interaction and drinking coffee with colleagues ultimately made me feel better, even though it was less productive. For some, the office is a haven, particularly if you factor in the not-so-fun commute. In addition, staying late in the office was the physical proof that I was dedicated and committed and work would get done, right? And as an added bonus: I could now make fun of the slackers who were working from home. Joy o' joy.

My perception started to change when my amount of business travel increased significantly. Now I was obligated to work regardless of where I was. I needed that time in the hotel to get things done while meeting during working hours. And guess what? When jetlag wakes you up in the middle of the night, you are not going to be in a chirpy state of mind to throw on a tie and suit before you get to your emails.

Having more employees approach me with the possibility of working remotely, I decided to compare my previous views to more fact-driven opinions. Based on the model by Daniel Kahneman, Dan Lovallo and Olivier Sibony and taking into account their HBR article, _The Big Idea: Before You Make that Big Decision..._,[1] I wanted to make sure my previous decisions were not made out of mere perceptions, self-interest or group thinking. I also wanted to make sure I did not fall for confirmation bias and exclude a viable alternative to being more productive. Finally, I started to realize that not considering remote work would likely expose me to competitor neglect. My peers in other companies were attracting talent with the remote-working model. Last but not least, I was denying myself and the company accessibility to a diverse team.

The results underlined my suspicions to be true. Study after study indicated that working remotely not only increases productivity but also contributes significantly to a company's bottom line through savings on office space, materials, insurance and other items. Another daunting fact is that remote workers are happier! Could it be that some people are less stressed when in a non-office environment and are not locked inside 5 x5 cube walls? It dawned on me that I might have made location a priority over hiring the best talent because they were not willing or able to move. I certainly begrudged the talented people who left my team to move to a different location when location is not really an issue anymore.

A change of mind was in order and I encourage all office people and their managers to reexamine their priorities. Would you rather have a superstar on your team who works remotely or are you willing to settle for local availability of resources? That is not to say that you cannot find great local talent, but the best are typically courted by companies from – you guessed it – anywhere. Meeting tools, methods of communication and accessibility are certainly no longer issues, either. So, there I had it.

I have tried to shine a light on working remotely from all angles and invite you along on my journey through my following posts. In the meantime, comments and opinions are very much always welcome.

(Visit www.beattheratrace.com to get access to my recently published book: STOP Applying for Jobs and have Recruiters Come to You (12 proven Steps for Getting Your Dream Job on LinkedIn Delivered to You.) It is available for FREE. If you feel compelled to purchase it on Amazon, proceeds will be used for further research and in support of charitable organization focusing on educational purposes.

1

HOW TO KNOW IF REMOTE WORK IS RIGHT FOR YOU

Working from home is the dream for many current office bees. The allure of setting your own workspace, the relative quiet and the potential for flexibility are like a siren song for some nine-to-fivers. And with studies looking at just how many hours in a day are spent on 'empty labor,' you might have an easier time than ever convincing an employer that remote work is best for everyone concerned. But are you a good fit for telecommuting? And is your position one that could easily be converted to a remote job? Here are a few questions to help you figure out if remote work is right for you.

- Why are you interested in remote work?

Are you looking at this as an opportunity to do two jobs at once? It's often a bad idea to assume that you can be a full-time parent and a full-time remote employee at the same time. Many parents who work from home still send their children to daycare during work hours at least part of the week to maintain a boundary between their jobs and their personal lives.

- What space do you have to work in?

As a follow-up to this question, is your space tidy, private and does it facilitate concentration? It's difficult to get things done with a disorganized desk at the office, but imagine the stress of trying to work in a messy apartment. When you work from home, chores such as doing the dishes and sweeping the floors may seem like productive tasks. It's easy to feel accomplished when you end the day with a tidy house--but an untouched work to-do list.

- How much of your day do you currently spend with other people?

It's much easier to get an idea of how you'll respond to a situation if you compare similar environments. Do you currently spend large parts of your workdays on your own? Hating the noise of a loud or distracting office isn't automatically the same as loving endless silence. It's often a good idea to test the waters with remote work by first doing a trial period. Discuss working from home on Fridays with your manager and try to become aware of how you feel on those days.

- Do you consider yourself more introverted or extroverted?

Again, there's no wrong answer here. You needn't feel like being an extrovert automatically rules out telecommuting. It just means you'll need to stay ahead of feelings of loneliness or being left out. Additionally, there's some interesting research on how motivation affects workplace procrastination. Are you intrinsically or extrinsically motivated?

- Is this a long-term job or a stepping stone?

If you're in this position for the foreseeable future with your company (however long that may be) then you may have an easier time networking. You can strategically connect with the people who will facilitate your advancement up the ranks. You can make it a point to go into the office for specific events. If, however, you're not married to your company, networking may become very difficult. Remote work can be isolating in that way. You might not hear about many of the opportunities being tossed around at the water cooler at the office. *Did you hear rival company X is hiring for Y?* Remember, though, that proving your competence with remote work now may make it easier to work from home in the future.

- How effective are you at written communication?

Do you ever have one of those little offhand questions pop up at work? Something that's too small to be considered important but not completely insignificant? You're unlikely to want to pick up the phone any time you need one of these questions answered.

This means you'll need some effective written communication skills. That includes being both accurate and concise.

• Are you willing to learn new tech?

If your employer doesn't already use a tool to manage tasks and communication for remote workers, they likely will in the future. It's common for organizations to cobble together tools or try new ones altogether, making the learning curve much steeper for the remote worker. Cloud-based tools can have complicated ownership rules, and you have to stay on top of updates or set notifications.

• How confident are you in your ability to drive your own schedule?

Some people thrive in situations where they're able to self-direct their days. Others fall off the productivity bandwagon without top-down management. Neither of these two individuals is in the wrong, they just have different needs.

• Do you currently have a daily routine?

If you're regularly shifting work around (think coming in late and then staying late) due to oversleeping, you may struggle with remote work. It's easy to promise yourself and your manager you'll be equally available throughout the day if you work from home, but the reality is your current habits will often dictate your future ones. And while you might be able to swing that later shift at work when you come in to the physical office, it may eventually erode trust with your employer in a remote work situation.

• Are you prone to overworking?

On the flip side of poorly-managed schedules is the *always on-call* remote employee. Do you answer calls at six o'clock in the morning from clients and manage a crisis that crops up at eight o'clock that same evening? It can be difficult to shut off, power down and disconnect from work if you're remote. This is especially true if you get notifications, emails, texts and calls on your personal electronic devices. You may need to set firm boundaries or simply come to terms with being more available for work.

• Do you have the tools you need to work remotely?

And do you have a backup plan for if and when they break down, or otherwise become unusable? There's nothing worse than having a full day ahead of you and a dead phone or a blue-screened laptop. Having a backup laptop may become more critical when working from home.

• Do you consider yourself forgetful?

This isn't the kiss of death, but rather an opportunity to determine the best workflow and tools to stay on top of your to-do list. As soon as a new task is assigned, it's important to physically add it to a written or electronic task manager. Your goal is to avoid having to be told more than once about an assignment. You want to prove to your boss you're effective at getting the job done.

• How do you respond to critical feedback from managers?

Written communication comes with many flaws, some of which you cannot personally solve. Perhaps your teammate, direct manager or boss has a curt or direct form of communicating feedback. Some people prefer negative information to be cushioned with praise. Others are fine with a short-and-to-the-point response. In many situations, the only thing you'll have control over is how you choose to respond to feedback.

• Are you a critical team member?

If your position currently deals with time-sensitive issues, you may have a harder time convincing an employer to let you work remotely. Even if that's not the case and it won't be any more difficult to reach you by phone, the assumptions higher-ups make about your accessibility still matters. Remote work may not be in the cards for now, but you can always reassess in the future.

• Have you met with your manager to discuss remote work?

Managers often have good insight into your personal strengths and weaknesses. They'll also be able to point out the parts of your job that could be difficult to complete remotely. In the end, this is the most important step toward working from home. If you still feel confident in your decision to work remotely and you're convinced it's now a good option for you, it may be time to approach your employer and make the move to working remotely.

How to Know if Remote Work is Right for You:

☐ Think about exactly why you're interested in remote work

Notes:

☐ Consider your workspace

Notes:

☐ Estimate how much of your day is spent around others

Notes:

☐ Determine how introverted or extroverted you are

Notes:

☐ Think about your five-and-ten-year plans at this company

Notes:

☐ Consider your strengths in written communication

Notes:

☐ Understand your willingness to learn new technology

Notes:

☐ Think about how much you're able to drive your own schedule

Notes:

☐ Create your daily routine

Notes:

☐ Keep track of how much overtime you work

Notes:

☐ Make a list of the tools you'll need to work remotely

Notes:

☐ Recognize your weaknesses

Notes:

☐ Understand how you respond to critical feedback from managers

Notes:

☐ Be aware of special considerations if you're regarded as a critical team member

Notes:

☐ Meet with your manager to discuss remote work

Notes:

2

EXPLORING DIFFERENT TYPES OF REMOTE WORK

The term *Remote Work* gets thrown about quite a bit in conversations about the modern workforce. From people craving a traveling lifestyle to retirees want a little extra cash for their hobbies, the idea has grown to encompass many different jobs. With all these types of remote work available, it's important to narrow in on exactly what your expectations are before diving in. You'll need to become fluent in the terminology, using terms like *independent contractor* and *diversified remote worker*. What's more, you'll need to determine what you're capable of taking on and how well that matches with a prospective job. Together, we'll explore the most common types of remote work out there today.

Full-Time Remote Worker

Ah yes, working at home full-time is one of the most coveted types of remote work. It's easy to think of this as nearly identical to your typical office job, where you come in for eight hours and work a full day alongside your colleagues -- sans the *coming in* part of the equation. You're likely expected to be present at your computer and phone at the same time as your company's other employees. You'll probably attend meetings virtually. You can often expect a salaried position with benefits. And, if you're employed by a larger company, you might even travel a few times a year to the headquarters for events.

Some organizations will hire employees on a full-time basis based on this type of remote work right off the bat. In that case, the expectations and support for this role are likely to be well-established. But what about converting to a remote position? Many people are eventually able to switch over to working from home once they've established their presence in the workplace. It requires trust from management, a solid plan and building up the necessary resources. You might want to prepare a convincing argument when attempting this route, as many employers still balk at this type of remote work. As a research paper highlighted on HBR.org from Stanford's Dr. Nicholas Bloom reveals, telecommuting can in fact cost less and improve productivity [1].

Keep in mind that full-time remote work may not be for everyone. There may be some unavoidable physical aspects of your job. Perhaps you'd struggle with significantly less day-to-day human interaction. Even an unreliable internet connection could reduce your options here. Take a look at this **checklist on how to know if remote work is right for you** if you've decided to explore this as an option.

Full-Time Freelancing or Gig-Based Work

Next up is also a full-time type of remote work. As Orly Lobel has written about extensively, freelancing is increasingly common in the emerging gig-based economy [2]. According to the Bureau of Labor, some of the most common fields for this type of employment right now include arts and design, programming and tech and media and communications. With each of these, the work is easily done from a home office or off-site. There's often little need for face time and interviews likely consist of proof-of-work portfolios.

The downside to this type of remote employment is pretty obvious. Without guaranteed long-term employment, more of your time is spent obtaining new contracts. Your income can fluctuate, and you'll need to plan for your own taxes, health insurance and retirement. The flexibility you get in return, however, is worth it to many people.

The benefits to employers are vast for contract-based work. They assume less liability in the long run. Plus, they can hire the perfect person for a highly specific job, using laser-like accuracy to solve a problem or improve the bottom-line. However, they may need to accept that the use of freelancers means the lack of commitment is a two-way street. That's not to say companies should expect poor work from contract employees, only that they may not be able to retain the best remote freelancers at the end of a contract without a fight. After all, gig-based workers chose this lifestyle for a reason.

Diversified Remote Worker

Another type of remote work is the *diversified* or part-time remote employee. This position fills in a bit of the gaps between the first two options above. A company may have needs that require a substantial amount of time spent on-site, but it can still allow the employee plenty of remote work. This is certainly not location-independent, but it does allow for flexibility on both sides. It's often a great option for parents who benefit from the extra hours not spent commuting to and from the office.

The Side Job

This is probably the most recognized type of remote work by Millennials today. With slow wage growth and larger than ever student debt, many young professionals turn to alternative means of making money. Moonlighting is a great way to increase your take-home pay if you can't get that promotion you've been gunning for. And with the advent of single-job sites like Upwork and Fiverr, it's easy to connect skills with tasks.

There are few downsides to a good side-hustle (except maybe fewer nights with your Netflix queue.) You can pick up small jobs when you have the time and skip it if things get busy at your 9-to-5. Taxes may get a little bit interesting come springtime, but many find it's worth the hassle for the extra income. Side jobs can come with some unexpected advantages, too. Some might allow you to spread your creative wings in ways you're not able to in your full-time job. Others give you experience in a new field. You can even try out a new job like you would a pair of jeans at the mall. If they don't fit quite right? No harm, no foul.

Remote Business Owners

The last type of remote work we'll cover here are remote business owners. Similar to other types of virtual employment, this has the added layer of employing other telecommuters. In fact, you might even hire any of the above types of remote workers yourself! As with any business owner, you'll have different responsibilities and rewards. You might need to decide on a company-wide communication system, learn how to handle disputes between employees virtually and manage a team of telecommuters. It's not for the faint of heart, but those who thrive in the role never want to leave it.

As with any type of employment, remote work comes in many forms. And just like any other workplace, each remote worker will have a different role and experience. With today's shifting employment environment, it's not surprising to find yourself shifting between the different types of remote work throughout your career. The best way to navigate them is, as always, to gather as much information as possible before making critical decisions. Don't let fear stop you from exploring your options. You might be surprised at what you find out there.

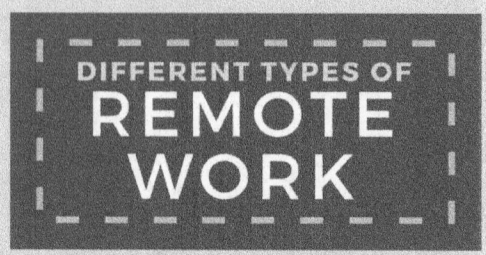

FULL-TIME REMOTE EMPLOYEE

Salary & benefits, often 40 hours per week with a set schedule

FULL-TIME FREELANCER

Gig-based, often with flexible hours

DIVERSIFIED REMOTE WORKER

Part remote, part on-site employment, varies from company to company

THE SIDE JOB

Gig-based, flexible hours Often driven through freelancing sites

REMOTE BUSINESS OWNER

High time investment, potential for a high payoff, employs other remote workers

Chapter References

[1] Kahneman D, Lovallo D, Sibony O; HBR reprint R1106B, The Big Idea: Before You Make that Big Decision...

[1] Bloom N, Liang J, Roberts J, Ying ZJ (2013) Does Working from Home Work? Evidence from a Chinese Experiment (NBER Working paper no. 18871).

[2] Lobel, O. The Gig Economy & the Future of Employment and Labor Law, 51 U.S.F. L. Rev. 51, 61 (2017)

(You have access to my recently published book: *STOP Applying for Jobs and have Recruiters Come to You (12 proven Steps for Getting Your Dream Job on LinkedIn Delivered to You*. It is available for FREE. If you feel compelled to purchase it on Amazon, proceeds will be used for further research and in support of charitable organizations focusing on educational purposes.)

3

6 COMMON MYTHS ABOUT TELECOMMUTING

With more Americans than ever working from home, it's important to separate fact from fiction on how remote employment functions. This can apply both to how it works for the company in question and how telecommuting affects individual employees. The larger the corporation, the more layers of management, which translates into lower risks borne across the business, but also more chances for a mismatch of expectations. We'll go over some of the common myths about working remotely, and address at least a *few* potential problems.

Remote Workers are Less Engaged

This myth is almost too easy to disprove. There's been plenty of research over the past couple of decades on how telecommuters are often *more* engaged employees [1], according to HBR.org. Think of all the ways you can waste your day surrounded by coworkers. There's the standard watercooler talk, as well as the endless meetings [2] covered in the MIT Sloan Management Review.

When you're all in the same location, it's easy to think getting everyone in a room together may solve any issues that arise. The truth of the matter is in smarter communication, not more of it. The minor hurdle of having to jump on a conference call or video chat or sending an email can potentially mean employees start to rethink how they communicate about projects. Is this something that you can actually handle on your own? Can you condense your questions into meaningful but compact ideas? If you've ever been in a classroom with too many people trying to sound like they did the required reading, you may find out quickly that the loudest voice in a meeting isn't necessarily the most well-informed one. Targeted communication, like the type you often see with remote employees, is a good way to strike the right balance between wasting time with disengaged employees and being too hands-off.

Reduced Productivity with Remote Work

Related to the last point about employee engagement is the idea that remote workers are less productive than their office bee counterparts. Ask anyone who's been telecommuting for a few years about their work-life balance, and you'll soon find that they're just as committed, if not more so, to being productive parts of the whole. Harvard Business Review looked at one compelling study on productivity [3] from Stanford Economics Professor Nick Bloom [4]. People who work from home appear to perform better on defined success metrics and they know it. Without a frustratingly long commute and the distractions of an office, these highly-engaged employees simply get more stuff done every day.

Remote Employees are Difficult to Contact

Many employers worry that their more time-sensitive positions aren't well-suited for telecommuting. After all, if your employee isn't sitting in their cubicle for eight hours a day, you can't guarantee you'll be able to reach them, right? In a TINYpulse survey [5], researchers found that though contact with management may decrease for some employees, this actually reflects a lower need for the contact in the first place. Though you might not be speaking daily, you're still checking in when you need to. This lower contact rate seems to improve general satisfaction on both ends.

Data Safety

It's easy to think that just because your employees are on the work network that the entire system is safer overall. The truth is larger corporations already rely on cloud-based systems--ones with the same vulnerabilities at home as well as in the office. The most common cause of security breaches is human error [6]. This includes downloading items that shouldn't be downloaded, clicking on links in spam emails and visiting unsafe sites. Think of the enormous Yahoo data breach that happened in 2016. It all started with a phishing attempt on an employee with the right credentials. Proper training on phishing is one of the most important ways companies can protect themselves from these attacks, rather than shutting down telecommuting options for everyone.

Less Respect for Remote Workers

There's still plenty of stigma still associated with people who work from home, but with the meteoric rise we mentioned earlier, this myth is ever-so-slowly losing its grip. Friends may still assume you'll be free to pick them up from the airport, join them for happy hour every day or even take care of children while being able to telecommute. The truth is many remote workers, though they may have a more flexible schedule, still put in just as much, if not more, daily effort. Remember the increased productivity we talked about? Those who telecommute often worry about the reverse problem of always appearing available to their employers, even after their regular work day is done.

Since this one isn't a myth, per se, it's important to look at the ramifications of this imbalance in how employees are viewed. In fact, remote workers will often go above and beyond to prove their worth – even more so than their office-based counterparts.

Complete Independence

All right, so this one can certainly vary between fields and for specific employers. In general, the assumption that remote employees somehow get to have complete independence from the daily grind of responsibilities is completely unmerited. They're often putting in overtime, working weekends or make themselves available outside of their normally-scheduled hours to accommodate their employers.

If the company has regular meetings remote employees telecommute into, they'll be there. If they have to be ready for clients in different time zones, they're up and ready to go early in the morning or late into the evening. Many of the same constraints which apply in the office often still hold sway for those working from home, simply for practical reasons. It's important for those considering remote work to know they may not have as much flexibility in the timing of their work as they do in the location. Mismatched expectations on either the part of the employer (who may expect too much) or the employee (who may expect too little) can sour the working relationship irreparably.

Always remember each person's experience with remote work is individual and multifaceted. Though these are some general myths, they may ring true for some telecommuters. Statistics can only tell us so much about the overall situation of people working from home.

Chapter References

[1] Edinger, S. Why Remote Workers Are More (Yes, More) Engaged (2012). *Harvard Business Review (Reprint Number H0099S)*.

[2] Scott, CW. The Science and Fiction of Meetings (2007). *MIT Sloane Review (Reprint Number 48207)*.

[3] Bloom, N. To Raise Productivity, Let More Employees Work from Home (2014) *(Reprint Number F1401D)*.

[4] Bloom N, Liang J, Roberts J, Ying ZJ (2013). Does

working from home work? Evidence from a Chinese experiment (NBER Working paper no. 18871).

[5] Likavec C, Olaya M, Wang D (2016). Surprising Differences in Workplace Happiness & Relationships (TINYpulse).

[6] Sharma, V (2017). Why do data breaches happen? (USC Marshall School of Business).

4

REMOTE WORK AND THE BOTTOM LINE

Much of the emphasis in discussions on remote work centers around how telecommuting can improve the lives of employees. While this is certainly a big part of the decision in switching to part or full-time remote employment, employers need to consider the bottom line. The good news is that, in many cases, employees working from home can be a boon to the company.

Increased Productivity and Engagement

The oft-cited work by Stanford's Nick Bloom [1] shows there's a bump in productivity when workers are able to work from home. What does that mean for the company? A 2016 Gallup Poll shows engaged employees produce higher quality work, fewer errors and even less internal theft [2]. It's easy to see how having fewer distractions around you can foster the right environment to focus on projects.

The Bureau of Labor Statistics has taken a deep dive into

productivity in the American workforce. Alongside an increase in telecommuting came a small – but very real – uptick in productivity. The ripples of changes like this can be felt across the entire economy of one of the largest countries across the globe.

Going Green

Do you find that your business is in the public eye regularly? Do you *want* it to be? Take a look at companies focused on cleaning up their act (literally). Whether you currently struggle with adhering to guidelines and recommendations for being environmentally friendly or you want to appeal to a specific audience, going green can be a great public-relations move. Based on an analysis of data from the 2005-2016 American Community Survey conducted by GlobalWorkplaceAnalytics.com, remote workers may help reduce greenhouse gas emissions by as much as 54-million tons each year.

Between reducing the number of cars on the road, to eliminating the need for larger office spaces, to digitizing forms of communication, remote work can have a huge positive impact on the planet. Consumers for whom this is a key deciding factor in purchasing appreciate moves like this, as well.

A More Reliable Workforce

Modern employment practices simply cannot rely on an always-present workforce. With vacations, sick time, parental leave and more, there are plenty of reasons your employees might need days (or weeks, or months) off.

Telecommuting has been estimated to reduce unscheduled absences by 63%. When an employee doesn't have to technically even get out of bed to hop on their laptop, the mental burden of coming "into the office" is much lower.

Any business owner or manager knows how costly unscheduled absences are. Larger companies may be able to absorb these issues more easily, but a small business has to juggle a smaller number of employees. Maybe it's even the owner who's stuck covering the added workload. If the work can be done from home, however, you may just find yourself with an overfilled plate a little less often.

Happier Remote Workers

That same study from Nick Bloom above [1] took a look into employee happiness for remote workers. Unsurprisingly, people reported higher job satisfaction. When employees feel comfortable in their position, they're less likely to jump ship, leaving you without a critical role filled for however long it takes to find their replacement. Between headhunting and recruiting, as well as training for their new role, this hiccup can lead to a big hit to the bottom line.

Remote work options also have one added bonus going for the company in terms of worker retention. It's simply not available everywhere. You can get a leg up on your competitors by providing something they don't have. Potential employees generally consider this benefit when applying to (or choosing to leave) a company. Stay ahead of the curve and get the very best new recruits.

This is especially true in larger metropolitan areas. With the steady rise of housing costs pushing families farther out of the city, commutes are getting longer and traffic worse. After a long car ride in bumper-to-bumper traffic in the morning, that email from your friend who works in HR at a remote-friendly business may seem even more appealing.

Decrease Discrimination

The Brookings Institute has previously written on how inflexible employment might be driving women out of certain types of professions [3]. Surveys show that employment which allows for more flexible telecommuting options is more appealing to women. But what's the benefit of a diverse workforce? It encourages daily innovation and high-quality candidates for positions when hiring. Having additional perspectives available during meetings and brainstorming sessions will allow for bigger and better ideas.

While having a screen between two people over the internet can be a recipe for disaster for strangers, it may be a perk for employees. Internal biases may not come into play as frequently when most communication is done over email, Slack or cloud-based communication. With a proper structure in place to handle the mediation of workplace issues, it may be easier to get everyone to fit together comfortably. In telecommuting situations, if two employees rarely see eye-to-eye, they won't be running into one another in the hallway at work. Wouldn't it be nice to avert some of those nastier HR disasters?

In addition to discrimination based on race, sex and gender identity, there's an entire category of workers who regularly encounter issues with office work – those with physical disabilities. While it's an important part of the

American ethos to make the workplace accessible for as many people as possible, disabled individuals may particularly benefit from remote work options. This can give them access to any supplies or modified setups they need in the comfort of their own home. They won't need to figure out complicated transportation. In fact, offering telecommuting may make your business more appealing to an even larger pool of highly-qualified applicants.

With every business-related decision impacting the future of your company, there must be a cost-benefit analysis. Some of these are quantitative costs with concrete dollar and cent figures attached to them. Others are qualitative and require more complicated deep-dives into their meaning. The decision to offer remote work options for employees is a big one, but we argue it can have many positive impacts on company growth and achievement. The key is to know what your company's values are and determine how to best structure your workplace to fit your goals. With careful planning and execution, many companies will benefit from the addition of telecommuting.

REMOTE WORK
AND THE BOTTOM LINE

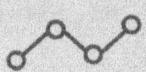

HIGHER PRODUCTIVITY

Remote workers show higher engagement, which leads to higher productivity

BALANCING ACT

Optimal engagement happens when employees spend 60 - 80% of their time working remotely

DAILY PROGRESS

Remote workers are more likely to report having productive days, especially compared to those who work from home less often

FACE TIME

If your company's structure can support it, spending 20% of their time in-office is the sweet spot for remote workers

$11,000 PER PERSON

The typical employer will save $11,000 per person per year switching to remote employment

Data sourced from GlobalWorkplaceAnalytics.com & Gallup

Chapter References

[1] Bloom N, Liang J, Roberts J, Ying ZJ (2013). Does working from home work? Evidence from a Chinese experiment (NBER Working paper no. 18871).

[2] Dvorak, N & Kruze, WE (2016). Managing Employee Risk Requires a Culture of Compliance. (Gallup).

[3] Sawhill, IV (2016). The gender pay gap: To equality and beyond (*Social Mobility Memos*).

5

HOW TO CONVERT A POSITION TO REMOTE ONLY

The term **telecommunication** dates back to the 1973 book *Telecommunications-Transportation Tradeoff: Options for Tomorrow* [1]. At the time, Jack Nilles was working hard on a communications system for NASA. Since then, the idea has expanded and grown to include a wide range of work-from-home arrangements between employers and employees. In today's highly-digitalized era, it has become easier than ever to hire someone (or be hired yourself) without ever seeing the other person in the flesh. Many jobs immediately lend themselves to remote work, like those in sales or writing. Others have had to wait for some of the more recent advancements in technology. If you're ready to take the dive – either as an employee trying to convert to a telecommuting position or as an employer attempting to offer employees the option to go remote – here are a few points to consider.

The Costs of Office Space

If you're a larger corporation or one which interacts with clients regularly, you certainly need some amount of office space. On the other hand, consider how much those desks, chairs and cubicles cut into the bottom line. In a city like New York, the average annual cost of renting office space is nearly 15-*thousand* dollars per employee. And while cities like Atlanta clock in at a much more manageable $4K, that's still money which could be spent on other goals within the company.

There are a few additional costs associated with the physical building where your employees work. Whether it's an employer perk or the employee footing the bill, public transportation and parking costs are a factor here. For the worker, they can save on gas, maintenance and even extend the life of their vehicle by a few years if they're putting fewer miles in it every day. As for the employer, they can concentrate on more important business decisions without having to constantly account for the limitations imposed by the physical space they inhabit. Converting on-site employees into full-time remote workers may open up room for innovation and scaling.

Identify Your Key Players

When transitioning employees from a brick-and-mortar setup to a fully-remote situation, you'll need to start with the most reliable people as your bedrock. If this is their first time working from home, you may need to help them through the transition period a bit more than you might expect. On the flip side of this equation, if you're going to be transitioned into a fully-remote job, try to identify the key people you'll need to reach out to for help if (and when) you need it. It's a good idea to dip your toes into the water by first working from home a few days a week. Ideally, rotate through the days of the week so you can identify any snags or needs that will have to be filled in your absence.

As an employer, you'll need to make sure your remote employee knows who their points of contact are. They need a direct manager, whether that's you or someone else, and they'll need to know what their role may be in managing others. It needs to be very clear from the outset that, although they're not physically present, anyone to whom they delegate work needs to treat emails and tasks from the telecommuter seriously. If your company has a human resources department, you'll need to make sure the employee is aware of their ability to contact them. In addition, let them know about any confidentiality rules surrounding certain types of communication.

Identify Your Tools

Your company likely already utilizes a full suite of tools to accomplish their organizational goals. Whether it's the email server used, project management software, the calendars enlisted to keep important dates straight or the complex databases store sensitive information, access to these tools are necessary for a remote employee's success.

With the advent of so many tools created to connect

people across far distances, more and more workplaces are considering making these switches. Higher education is one of those sectors that's been playing with the idea of remote employees recently [2]. Beyond email and messenger applications, there's video chats and conference calling. Task managers are becoming more prevalent as well, with free resources like Asana and Todoist. They can provide the necessary structure which might be lacking for remote employees who don't go in to work every day. Cloud-based information is another huge step for employers looking to take some or all of their workforce remote. Google Drive is a great (and also free) example of this. Dropbox, Box, and other more secure systems can help protect data, as well.

For employees going remote, the tools they need may look a little different. They'll obviously have to have a higher-quality computer or laptop, a good internet connection and a reliable phone. On top of that, they may also want to look into carving out a space in their home that's just for work. This may not be feasible for everyone (especially if they're in a high-cost city) but it's a good way to create a more structured work area.

Start Small

As Mahlon Apgar outlined in their *Organizational Culture* article in Harvard Business review two decades ago [3], starting small may be a good idea for both employees and employers switching to a remote workplace.

For employers, this could mean experimenting out with a smaller group of less-critical employees. They may be less vital for operations, so the experiment is relaxed as it takes its course. For employees, this might look like starting to work from home a few days a week rather than the entire week. Both of these tactics will allow the company to identify and plug any holes that arise. Is there a lack of communication between critical parties? Are necessary tasks going undone? Expect these kinds of hiccups and have everyone prepared to pitch in to fix them. Organizations will likely need to devote some extra resources to these issues (hey, you could use that money you're saving on office space!) so don't be surprised if initial tests with remote working don't go off without a hitch.

Scalability is often the end goal here, giving companies the ability to keep a larger workforce with lower operating costs. A larger sales force may bring more leads, for example, increasing the company's monthly income substantially.

The decision to convert employees to remote-only positions is a weighty one. For employers, the potential downside may seem large and looming. For employees, the structure of coming into the office each day may hold a certain appeal. Done carefully, a transition to telecommuting can benefit both parties equally, leading to more productivity and increased happiness.

Chapter References

[1] Nilles JM. *Telecommunications-Transportation Tradeoff: Options for Tomorrow* (1973).

[2] Reshma PS, Acharya S & Aithal PS. *Relevance of On-*

Line Office Administration Through Working from Home in Future Education System (2015); International Journal of Application or Innovation in Engineering & Management (IJAIEM), Volume 4, Issue 4, pp. 44-53, ISSN 2319 - 4847.

[3] Apgar M. *The Alternative Workplace: Changing Where and How People Work* (1998); Harvard Business Review.

6

6 WAYS TO PROMOTE INCLUSIVITY WITH REMOTE WORKERS

With remote workers, inclusivity can make or break your company. Whether you have a 100% remote team or a blended workplace, you'll need to adapt to the unique issues which can arise. As Joseph Grenny and David Maxfield outlined in their analysis of research in the Harvard Business Review [1], remote workers are prone to feeling left out and shunned. That lack of engagement can have downstream effects on productivity and employee retention over the long run, as well. Below are some of the best ways to promote inclusivity for remote workers.

Build Effective Communication Channels

When melding telecommuting and office-based employees, effective communication is key. Teams working on the same project need to be able to plan together, give regular progress updates and make dynamic changes as issues arise. This isn't just a technological solution, either. While a dedicated chat application is a vital component, it's not sufficient for success.

The last thing you want productivity-wise is to have what could be a simple conversation take hours to hammer out over written communication. One person initiates, another responds after lunch, the first agrees by the end of the day, and then neither can get started on the real work until the next business day. Emails by nature have a lower urgency than chats, so a good solution may be to set up a dedicated Slack channel or something similar. This has the added benefit of being an easily searchable record of conversations between employees for future reference. You'll also be joining the 72% of companies who use social tools for communication.

Set the Work Hours

While one of the main benefits of working from home might be the ability to set your own hours, it's a good idea as an employer to set limits on how employees may interpret this. Unless projects can be tackled entirely independently from one another, you'll likely need to have team members overlap some time in their work day. Perhaps you can focus on facilitating recurring meetings, or simply make sure remote and in-office employees are always available between a specific set of hours each day.

Try to avoid getting too broad in laying down the law, however. If you simply have the same eight hours set aside every day, it's easy for employees to take you less seriously –

lleading to the opposite effect from what you're looking for as an employer. Just as in a normal workplace, remote workers can't be 'on' all the time. It's much better if teammates save up their relevant questions for a single Q & A session. This prevents constant context-switching for your employees, which can be difficult for some people.

Schedule Performance Evaluations

Remote employee performance reviews can come in many forms. Some workplaces prefer less formal regular check-ins, while others rely more heavily on structured annual evaluations. If your project managers aren't seeing their team members daily, they may be missing out on opportunities to course-correct through casual conversations. This doesn't need to be a problem without a solution, however. Scheduling check-ins on specified days of the week or month allows for those more casual nudges. It also prevents the negative cycle of fear that can develop if your management team only reaches out to employees when they've misstepped.

An effective performance evaluation starts with concrete goals and objectives. Both managers and employees will have a chance to prepare for each evaluation. It makes it easier to track progress over time if you're all using the same structure. Reviews shouldn't just be from higher ups on down, either. Ideally, remote workers will also get the opportunity to reflect on their relationship with those managers, both directly and to the overarching management team, where applicable. Peer-to-peer evaluations can also be enlightening.

Finally, make sure there's a follow-up plan in place to put any new suggested new paths moving forward into effect following an evaluation.

Audit Your Toolkit

From tools for communication to those for planning and list-making, it's likely your company has accumulated a wide range of apps and programs. Take some time to evaluate what your company uses and if there's any overlap between tools. If your employees have to constantly check multiple chat platforms, they're wasting their time and yours. Where necessary, condense everything into a single tool every employee uses, whether they're in the next cubicle over or a thousand miles away. This can help prevent remote employees from feeling excluded or singled out, and it promotes a streamlined process for everyone involved in a project.

If you're paying big bucks for monthly or annual subscriptions, this audit can also help you figure out the difference between the wheat and the chaff when it comes to effective tools. Ask your remote employees for an honest evaluation of their current programs and applications. See if there are any gaps that need to be filled or areas that could use a little less in the way of technological solutions.

Enable Chats During Meetings

One of the best tools your employees can take advantage of may very well be those chat tools we keep mentioning – but this time using them in meetings. It may feel a bit like interrupting while someone else is speaking in class, but the truth is, allowing a written chat during a video presentation could be the perfect solution to difficult problems. Employees can immediately raise questions to their colleagues. They will have the means to clarify points which are often otherwise solved at the water cooler in a more traditional workplace. Plus, this solution can offer even more inclusivity for hearing-impaired employees.

Encourage Personal Communication

This isn't an authoritarian workplace from the movies. It's a multifaceted company with living, breathing human beings. Make sure your remote employees know they can shoot the breeze a bit and actually get to know their coworkers. Obviously, you don't want an HR issue on your hands with inappropriate conversations, but make sure people have a chance to talk about something other than work tasks without fear of a reprimand. With much of their daily communication being written in the form of emails or chats, telecommuters may feel like they're being monitored. On top of that, it may feel awkward or uncomfortable to initiate these conversations when they're not face-to-face. Ice-breaker games get a bad rap, but they can really work to help build camaraderie between remote workers.

From an employer's perspective, promoting inclusivity for remote employees may feel more like a luxury than a necessity. If you want to build a team that works well together, you're going to eventually need to put the metaphorical ping-pong table in the break room.

PROMOTING INCLUSIVITY WITH REMOTE WORKERS

EFFECTIVE COMMUNICATION

72 percent of companies use social tools for communication between employees

SET WORK HOURS

Find the sweet spot between too broad and too narrow when it comes to setting expected available hours

EVALUATIONS

Schedule regular performance evaluations for both remote workers and their managers

AUDIT YOUR TOOLKIT

Evaluate what your company uses and ensure that everyone has access to the same tools

COLLABORATION

Encourage collaboration during video conferences by enabling chat boxes

GET PERSONAL

Encourage other employees to build camaraderie with remote workers

Chapter References

[1] Grenny J & Maxfield D. *A Study of 1,100 Employees Found That Remote Workers Feel Shunned and Left Out* (2017); Harvard Business Review.

7

5 STRATEGIES FOR NETWORKING WHEN YOU WORK REMOTELY

You can find plenty of definitions of *career networking* in business books and on job sites. Whether you look at networking as a series of exciting opportunities or onerous requirements, it's clear that this method of building up your personal resources is critical for success. With as much as 85% of jobs at a given company filled through networking, no one looking to advance in their career should take this tool lightly. Many in the business world would argue that effective networking cannot be achieved through a one-way street of favors. It's a give-and-take situation, where each person involved in the connection provides something useful for the other. Perhaps that's knowledge or material goods. It can even be simple camaraderie or advice. As Gianpiero Petriglieri at Harvard Business Review outlined in his deep dive on the topic [1], through building these relationships, you create a system – a network – of people you trust and who trust you back enough to vouch for you in the future.

Now that we're all hopefully on the same page with the value of networking, what are some of the unique challenges as it relates to remote workers? After all, the opportunity for incidental friendships and mentorships dwindles the less time you spend at a brick-and-mortar business. That makes the process of networking much more active for telecommuting employees. However, while there are plenty of issues, none are insurmountable.

Just Do It

As mentioned above, networking as a remote employee is a far more active verb in business. It's easy to write off as unnecessary invitations to come to work events or optional meetings, but they're a great way to get face time with your employers, managers and coworkers. If you've fallen into the habit of being a bit of a recluse, try to shake things up. Say yes to a holiday party. Offer to take a coworker out for dinner if they're in your home-base town. Get into the office occasionally – even if you don't have to.

Networking doesn't necessarily require in-person contact, though it's a great option if you have it. *Choosing* to actively build relationships with those you work with may require some extra effort, but it can be well worth it over time.

Topple Barriers

This advice comes from one of the oldest pieces of psychological truisms: how you perceive and handle obstacles in the way of your goals makes a huge difference in the final outcome. In other words, if you make it harder to do something, you're simply less likely to actually do it. Now, as a remote worker, some of the things standing in between you and your network may be unavoidable. Perhaps you live in a different city or you have specific disabilities that make physical meetings with others problematic.

Other issues are a bit self-inflicted, however. Maybe you're not so great at making time in your calendar for those optional meetings. Perhaps you dislike the chat program your company uses because you're not quite sure how it works. If there's something causing a hiccup in communication, see if you can prioritize fixing that in the near future.

Be Reliable

This isn't just referencing getting your work done in a timely manner. If you want to network, make sure others know when you're available to help them with a problem. These are excellent opportunities to provide information or assistance, thus opening up that two-way channel. Gratitude can go far when it comes to performance reviews and recommendations for a new job. Lending assistance gives the other person a concrete example to reference when building you up to a third party.

Depending on your individual work environment, this can also bleed into the personal realm, as well. If you have a friendly relationship with the other employees – or the employer – it can pay big dividends to act as a reliable friend. That isn't to say you should be overstepping work boundaries, but there's a happy medium which can be struck between standoffish and HR complaint.

Seek Outside Opportunities

So far, this advice has mainly focused on in-company networking for remote workers. However, there's a world of opportunities out there beyond your own place of employment. Social media and networking-specific events are great places to learn more about your business and see what other people are doing to succeed. Look up Facebook groups in your niche, or explore local Meetups. These are often geared specifically toward people with outside-the-box jobs or nonstandard employment such as remote work.

One of the added benefits of general networking is opening up space for lateral moves into other industries. For example, you may have excellent communication skills (for, say, for technical writing in the aerospace industry). Networking might help you find you the relationships you need to get a job in a different industry using those same skills in a different way.

Networking By Any Other Name...

The process of networking isn't always going to look like showing up to dedicated events ready to knock the socks off your next potential employer. It can also be doing small jobs as a freelancer or even volunteering your time to gain a new skill. You can get practice by exercising a lesser-used tool in your personal kit, grow your confidence in your own abilities and nurture relationships with others in a different field. It's no secret that employers are risk-averse when hiring new employees. As a remote worker, you may have the unique opportunity to provide useful work on the side in a field you're interested in, simultaneously showing your worth as a future employee.

Volunteering has an added component for remote workers when it comes to networking. Building out a resume with nonprofit work and other generous uses of your time looks great to current and future employers. It shows you're committed to the good work you're doing, regardless of monetary compensation. Many charitable organizations are always on the lookout for volunteers willing to perform skilled labor, allowing you to add to your repertoire over time without already having the experience.

If your workout class or cycling group happens to have a potentially useful connection, don't hesitate to reach out to him or her in friendship. Does the local community college allow outside speakers for group meetings? See if you can offer your knowledge and useful information to them. Joining friends at their conference or work party? Be as sociable as you're comfortable with and try to make at least one new acquaintance.

Networking can feel like a business-centric word, but for remote workers, it's really much more relationship-focused. Instead of treating coworkers in a transactional way, see what you have to offer them, and you'll often quickly find out what they can give back to you.

STRATEGIES FOR NETWORKING WHEN WORKING REMOTELY

JUST DO IT

The first step for effective networking is a simple one - knowing the importance of creating solid relationships

TOPPLE BARRIERS

Prevent unnecessary roadblocks in communication channels with coworkers

BE RELIABLE

Create dedicated channels and times for communications with coworkers, managers and employers

SEEK OUTSIDE OPPORTUNITIES

Social media and networking-specific events are great places to expand your network

NETWORK OUTSIDE THE BOX

Practice skills, gain confidence and meet new people in unorthodox networking situations

Chapter References

[1] Petriglieri G. To Take Charge of Your Career, Start by Building Your Tribe (2018). Harvard Business Review.

6 PERKS OF WORKING FROM HOME

If you've never worked from home before then the benefits might seem fairly straightforward, right? You avoid your commute, you skip out on the uncomfortable office chit-chat and you get to work all day in your PJs. While many of those are certainly true, there are some extras that even experienced remote workers may not have realized. Some will be things you experience every day that you take for granted, while others are the occasional benefit that really pack a punch.

Save Money On Your Commute

Crunching the numbers, you're looking at nearly $800 per year in combined commuting costs *per mile* that you live from work if you drive. That's taking into account the car payments, repairs and other incidentals that come along with a lengthy trip to and from the office each day. If you're more of a public transit kind of person, you're still looking at that monthly or annual pass to use the city bus system. Even biking to work requires some initial investment and maintenance costs.

There's a good reason why some workers are willing to take a pay cut to go remote. According to a study by Harvard Business review [1], hypothetical job-seekers are often unable to accurately evaluate just how much a longer commute affects their emotional, psychological and physical well-being into the future.

Work With People You Like

Just like your family, you don't exactly get to choose the people you work with in most cases. And while some remote workers may look around them and enjoy the silence, others really benefit from having others to work next to. Coworking spaces are a place where remote employees of disparate companies, freelancers, and similarly office-less people can work on their own projects in an office-like setting. According to another study by Harvard Business Review [2], about half of people sharing coworking spaces hang out outside of work.

You don't have to invest in one of these ventures to feel the benefits, either. Simply setting up 'work dates,' 'work parties' or 'crunch sessions' can help you feel less lonely as a telecommuter. You get the added bonus of choosing who you work next to, as well. And if you're not feeling social on that particular day? Curl up on the couch in your PJs and grab your laptop. It can be nice to not have to force human interactions based on everyone else's schedule for a third (or more) of your work week.

Optimize Your Work Environment

Do you get your best work done when you're jamming out to classical opera? Or do you like to work through a difficult problem out loud? When you work in an office, you often have to make compromises with your work space. Some companies can even be a little invasive on the desk or cubicle adornment rules. Wearing headphones for hours on end can be an uncomfortable solution to the pervasive silence, too. With remote workers, it's pretty obvious how you have a complete 180 from a restrictive workplace. Put on that vinyl record, put up that strange piece of artwork you got at your last convention, curse out loud at the third email you received about scheduling a doctor's appointment. The sky's the limit here (within reason, of course).

Tiny, Yet Time Consuming Chores

How long does it take for you to transfer a load of laundry from the washer to the dryer? Maybe five minutes, at most. Completing a full wash and dry cycle, on the other hand, can take hours. How about signing for a package at the door? Two minutes. Of course, having to stop by the nearest pick-up location for that package you missed during business hours takes significantly longer. These tiny tasks take up so little time, but they're spread out over full days or difficult to complete outside of your work hours – if you're at your office.

Getting these household chores out of the way when you have a moment before you make lunch means that evenings and weekends can be reserved for plans that are actually fun.

You're not stuck at home waiting for a buzzer to ding. You don't have to take precious vacation time just to be there for the plumber to show up. Depending on the work you do remotely, you likely don't have time for a deep clean of your bathroom during a conference call, but those small tasks that add up are amazing to knock out on a Tuesday afternoon.

Travel, Travel & More Travel

Did you know that it's about 20% cheaper to fly to your destination on a Thursday and return home on a Monday than it is to make the same trip Friday or Saturday? Remote employees who truly have the flexibility to work from anywhere can take advantage of this without wasting any of their time visiting family. If you take a trip to visit your parents on a Thursday evening and work from a local coffee shop (or even their living room) Friday and Monday during regular work hours, you get the benefit of all that time together without taking a single vacation day.

If you have room in the budget for it, you can even see about working abroad for a while. Plenty of countries around the world are set up to allow for longer stays with great internet access. Plus, there are quite a few interesting places that are only a few hours (plus or minus a day) off from American cities. You don't have to get a job teaching English in another country to experience life abroad.

Avoid Impulse Buys

Americans spend thousands of dollars each year on undrunk to-go coffee, convenience foods, lunches out and more.

While the specter of online shopping is still there at home for remote workers, most impulse shopping – around 70% – is actually on food. After a long day at work, the drive through line can beckon even the strictest of healthy eaters. Have a morning meeting? That AM java calling to you from the coffee shop around the corner is hard to resist. Let's not even get into how many times you forgot your lunch on the kitchen counter this month alone. It's easier to have a planned-out week when you have more control over what your day looks like. This, of course, has a snowball effect on things like your health as well. That fast food burger isn't doing your arteries any favors.

Most impulse shopping also involves taking advantage of a sale or special. In other words, those businesses need your eyes on their advertisements in the window or on billboards to reel you in.

The best part about working remotely is truly the flexibility. You have the power to make your work day look more or less like a standard 9 to 5. If you don't like something, you get to change it.

6 PERKS WHEN WORKING FROM HOME

SAVE MONEY ON YOUR COMMUTE

The average person spends nearly $800/year **per mile** that you live from work when driving

WORK WITH PEOPLE YOU LIKE

Choose who you sit next to each day, whether it's coworkers, friends or no one at all

OPTIMAL WORK ENVIRONMENT

Surround yourself with exactly what makes you feel most productive

TAKE ADVANTAGE

Tiny, yet time consuming chores are often spread out over hours or even days over the weekend -- but they can be knocked out any day of the week

TRAVEL

Your newly flexible schedule means that travel to visit friends and family or explore the world just got easier

NIX IMPULSE BUYS

kip the undrunk to-go coffee, convenience foods, lunches out and more when you avoid the commute to work

Chapter References

[1] Gino F, Staats B, Jachimowicz JM, Lee J & Menges JI. Reclaim Your Commute (2017). Harvard Business Review.

[2] King S. Coworking Is Not About Workspace — It's About Feeling Less Lonely (2017). Harvard Business Review.

9
HOW WORKING REMOTELY AFFECTS PRODUCTIVITY

With the ever-rising number of telecommuting employees, research in the past few years is intensely focusing on how working remotely affects productivity. And according to the studies, the key to higher output from workers may not be tips, tricks or hacks, but rather flexibility when it comes to where and when they work. Let's dig into some of the hard numbers to see exactly how that happens.

Increased Job Satisfaction

An analysis by Alan Felstead and Golo Henseke [1] in the journal *New Technology, Work and Employment* highlights the increased job satisfaction and job-related well-being for remote workers. While that in and of itself is an excellent goal for everyone involved, it also has downstream effects. Additional experimentation has shown that productivity may increase by as much as 20% for happy employees – an especially amazing fact compared to a GDP growth baseline of just a few percentage points. This isn't a passing trend, either, or one whose effects dissipate over time. Forbes reported that the stock prices of companies listed among Fortune's illustrious "100 Best Companies to Work For" rose 14% every year over the nearest decade measured, compared to the 6% average increase. There does seem to be a strong positive relationship between the happiness of employees and every measurable outcome for a company.

Fewer Distractions

When a standard office worker ponders what it might be like to work remotely, they may very well be imagining a day filled with distractions, household chores and more. The reality is that telecommuters report being able to complete more work over a smaller time frame. While there may be an adjustment period, people often settle into their own version of a perfect system. Whether that's an ideal desk setup, blasting classical music or simply having total silence, the flexibility means they get to experiment until they get things just right. Between meetings, conversations around the water cooler, gossip, demanding managers and other distractions, the office can easily become the most difficult place to get anything done.

Willingness to Work

It may not come as a surprise to learn that 52% of remote workers are less likely to take time off when they're sick as compared to their office counterparts. After all, there's not much of a chance of sneezing on anyone and they don't have to worry about just how red their nose looks. Really though, removing barriers to work like commutes and other frustrations means the impulse to just call out for the entire day is greatly diminished.

Even more surprising, nearly a quarter of telecommuters are willing to put in overtime to see a project through. This level of commitment can really help a smaller organization that's trying to get off the ground or a larger company that needs to hit their quarterly returns. In fact, surveys find that 80% of remote workers reported higher morale, which is in direct contrast to concerns over telecommuters feeling less connected to their projects and place in the company. Everyone wins when they're all on the same page in terms of cooperation and commitment.

Flexible Thinking

Have you ever had a fantastic idea come to you in the shower? We've all had those moments at the oddest times, and there's a good reason for it. The *right* kind of distractions – a nice shower or a walk with the dog, perhaps – allow our brains to disengage from useless thought patterns when we're trying to solve a difficult puzzle. It allows creativity to take control as the decision-making part of your brain is on a temporary hiatus. Having the boundaries between work and home life a little bit blurrier may allow people the flexibility they need to take action on those great ideas that come to them, no matter what time of day. We all know what happens to fleeting ideas if we allow them to float away without writing them down and starting on those first steps.

Reduced Stress

Hand-in-hand with job satisfaction is a reduction in the amount of stress people feel when they work from home. Over half of employees feel anxious about work, and that sentiment seems to be growing over time. Advice from Rich Fernandez [2] over at Harvard Business Review highlights the need for managers to take the stress of the employees under them seriously – or risk burnout. High stress can mean an increase in mistakes, more turnover with employees and lower productivity. For working parents, what they seem to want most to reduce stress seems to be a flexible working schedule, which telecommuting often provides.

Even worse, high-stress workplaces will eventually develop a poor reputation in their industry for chewing people up and spitting them out. They'll attract fewer highly-qualified candidates in a downward spiral that hurts everyone involved. Plus, anxiety can lead to many unexpected downstream effects for employees, such as health and relationship problems at home and at work.

Remote Workers Are Healthier

Speaking of better health, there are plenty of reasons to think that office job is killing you. Sitting has been touted as the new smoking, and while that sounds a bit dramatic, the numbers don't lie. It's easy to feel a little self-conscious regularly getting up and walking around your workplace. Maybe you're afraid your manager will think you're avoiding important work or that your fellow employees will become distracted with all that pacing. Working from home eliminates these issues. Plus, if you want to get in a workout at lunchtime, you no longer need to pretend those little wipes you keep in your gym bag are the same thing as a real shower.

It's not just physical activity, either. Research has found that people who *don't* telecommute [3] were at greater risk for conditions such as alcoholism and tobacco dependency. These can often translate into calling in sick or other long-term employment issues which can impact productivity. Mental health also plays a big role here, with a daily commute adding to the stress mentioned above. Office gossip and forced face-to-face interactions between employees who don't get along well can also be disruptive elements every day.

While it may not be the perfect solution for every person or industry, remote employment can be a real boon to workplace productivity. It creates major benefits with a bonus secondary perk – increased output.

Chapter References

[1] Felstead A & Henseke G (2017). Assessing the growth of remote working and its consequences for effort, well-being and work-life balance; *New Technology, Work and Employment*, 32:3.

[2] Fernandez R (2016) Help Your Team Manage Stress, Anxiety, and Burnout. *Harvard Business Review*.

[3] Henke RM, Benevent R, Schulte P, Rinehart C, Crighton KA & Corcoran M (2016). The Effects of Telecommuting Intensity on Employee Health; *Am J Health Promot.*, 30:8.

10

COMMUNITY & GLOBAL EFFECTS OF REMOTE WORK

Remote employment has shifted how individuals and companies think about jobs and business structures. As more and more industries are seeing an increase in the number of telecommuters in the past years and decades, more research is being done into the larger-scale effects. With millions of people skipping the normal nine-to-five in a cubicle, there are many ripples throughout the economy and society. Some are good, others are neutral and a few may be viewed as less than ideal. At the end of the day, it often comes down to looking at the pros and cons to see which wins out. Through most lenses, the good far outweighs the bad, with remote employment options on a community and global level.

Where People Live

How expensive is real estate in the biggest startup heavy cities? The median price of a single-family home in the Bay Area of California is $1,070,000. In Boulder, CO it's well over half-a-million dollars. New York and Seattle rank right up there, as well. What do all of these places have in common? Excellent job prospects that can fund those enormous mortgages and the inflated cost-of-living. The problems, of course, are manifold. Those with tech-industry jobs may be able to afford home prices in that range, but not everyone--even within a single family--can work in these jobs. Friction occurs as the wealth gap increases, creating ever-escalating issues for service industry employees, teachers, public workers and others. It's a problem without an obvious solution, so long as the jobs are location-dependent. With remote employment, you can have a company's computer programmers, writers and other location-independent roles spread across the country.

On top of cost of living, there are additional benefits to being able to work from anywhere. Research by Patrick Coate, Pawel Krolikowski and Mike Zabek [1] has shown that living near family can protect you from the financial consequences of job loss. Sudden unemployment can have negative and lasting effects on someone's future earnings due to the difficulty of job searching, lack of mentorship and unstable living situations. Having family nearby may greatly reduce these problems in the short-term, leading to prosperity in the long-term. Remote work allows younger people, especially, to remain close to the resources their parents can provide, bridging the gap created through unemployment. On top of that, retired parents can often help with childcare for single parents or dual-income households with kids, a considerable savings for young families.

This doesn't even take into account the emotional and mental benefits of simply being around the people you love.

Having a support system can make a huge difference in your life.

Family Life

Speaking of young families, remote workers often enjoy a level of flexibility that allows for an improved home life. Parents often cite having a flexible schedule as one of the most desirable perks in a work situation. Without a commute of their own, they're suddenly able to be there to load the kids onto the school bus or drive them to school themselves. They can more easily make it to a soccer game or dance recital after they clock out. When a child is sick, they're occasionally able to multitask with work and nursemaid duty. Telecommuting often allows parents to create a schedule which better fits the reality of raising kids in today's world.

Related to the first point, families can also choose where they live based on school districts instead of proximity to the office. This can have some serious knock-on effects as kids move through the different phases of education. If living in sunless Seattle isn't working out well for sensitive kids, remote working parents can pick up and move the family to perpetually sunny Phoenix.

Diverse Teams

Aside from benefits to your personal life, remote employment options also have some major pros for the workplace. Paul Gompers and Silpa Kovvali wrote in Harvard Business review [2] about how diversity improves the dynamics within organizations and teams. Along every concrete measurement in the venture capital industry, the more homogeneous the partners, the lower their investments performed. Essentially, when you keep hiring people who look, think and act like you, you're narrowing the range of creativity in your employees. People with different backgrounds have often been forced to solve problems – both professional and personal – in a variety of ways. They've also likely dealt with different issues over the years, creating a broader pool of experiences for them to draw upon later in life and in work.

Making positions remote-capable where possible can, when done correctly, increase diversity in your employee makeup. It won't happen on its own, but it's a great start. Look to expand along dimensions of race, ethnicity, gender, sexual orientation, socio-economic status, political views and anything else you can think of. A diverse team may need help meshing well, so be prepared to handle issues as they arise. The end result will more than justify the work involved.

New Support Industries

With the boom in remote work, there's been a rising tide of new needs for these telecommuters. Shared workspaces are popping up in larger cities and the company WeWork now owns more office real estate than anyone else in New York City. Taskmasters, to-do list apps and other productivity managers are huge for self-directed remote employees and freelancers to help manage their workloads. You can even get corporate-grade internet piped right to your living room.

While many economists may indulge in nail-biting prognostications over the future, it's clear the world is simply evolving alongside the changing needs of companies and modes of employment. Industries devoted to supporting the standard office work model may see a decline in profits as they move to adjust to the new norms. This is simply the normal groaning and grinding of the economy as it marches forward. The best part is that many of these new industries can themselves be remote employers, too. Support work is often location-independent, as are app-based jobs.

It's easy to fail to see the forest for the trees when it comes to tweaks to the economic landscape in a changing country or world. There will always be some amount of give and take as companies and individuals learn to accommodate new roles and dynamics in the work sphere. However, the impact telecommuting may have on a community is well worth the potential difficulties along the way. This global movement is opening doors in ways that will shape how we work in the years and decades to come.

COMMUNITY & GLOBAL EFFECTS OF REMOTE WORK

WHERE PEOPLE LIVE

With remote employment, you can have a company's computer programmers, writers and other location-independent roles spread across the country.

FAMILY LIFE

Remote workers often enjoy a level of flexibility that allows for an improved home life. Telecommuting can allows parents to create a schedule that better fits the reality of raising kids in today's world.

DIVERSE TEAMS

Diversity improves the dynamics within organizations and teams. Along every concrete measurement in the venture capital industry, the more homogeneous the partners, the lower their investments performed.

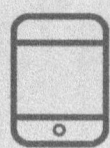

NEW SUPPORT INDUSTRIES

Task masters, to-do list apps and other productivity managers are huge for self-directed remote employees and freelancers to manage their workload.

Chapter References

[1] Coate P, Krolikowski P & Mike Zabek (2017). Parental Proximity and the Earnings Consequences of Job Loss; *Economic Commentary of the Federal Reserve Bank of Cleveland.*

[2] Gompers P & Kovvali S (2018). The Other Diversity Dividend; *Harvard Business Review.*

11

5 NECESSARY SKILLS FOR CURRENT OR ASPIRING REMOTE WORKERS

Remote work holds plenty of appeal for people. Between the flexible hours, the endless opportunity for travel and other great perks, telecommuting is certainly attractive for potential or current employees. But what do people want on the other side of that paycheck? There are a number of tangible and intangible factors that go into hiring the right person for a remote job. Beyond experience relevant to the role, working from home means honing a unique skill set that you can show off to future employers. Let's dive into some of those to see what you may already have nailed down – and what might still need a little bit of polishing.

Self-Motivation

Much as we'd all like to think of ourselves as exemplary employees, there will be days where the call of Twitter or the sports channel seems overwhelming. Being self-motivated isn't simply a personality trait, it's a muscle you must develop and strengthen over time. As Ayelet Fishbach described in their deep dive on self-motivation at work in Harvard Business Review [1], this ability is one of the key factors that elevates high-achieving professionals when compared to their peers.

If you're currently a remote worker, think about the parts of your day you enjoy. Perhaps you like reaching out to clients or researching specific topics. Maybe it's writing creative content that makes your heart sing. When you wake up every morning, remind yourself of the positive aspects of your work (as opposed to thinking of your to-do list as an endless litany of chores). Some people thrive off of an external reward system, so consider the types of milestones and the corresponding incentive you can give yourself. Of course, the flip side is loss aversion, where you take away something enjoyable if you're unable to complete your work.

Humility

That's right, let's talk about a big, old-fashioned slice of humble pie. Are you generally a very organized person? Do you only have to be told something once and you'll remember it? Are you reliable, responsible and every other positive R-sounding attribute? Being an army of one is great, but there will come a time (and it always does) when there is simply too much on your plate. Maybe your error is forgetting a smaller task or perhaps it's as large as missing a deadline.

With the self-directed nature of remote work, you're going to come face-to-face with the possibility of failure eventually. The thing is, as a telecommuter, no one around you sees your struggles on a daily basis. People who work from home often run somewhat independently from the rest of a team, and this can be both a blessing and a curse. Strong communication is going to come up again and again here, but nowhere is it more important than in self-preservation. Admitting fault or the inability to do a task is an uncomfortable but necessary skill for remote workers. With many managers operating under an out of sight, *out of mind* heuristic with their non-office-bound employees, it's easy to let difficulties like this slip through the cracks.

Organization

You have to have seen this one coming. Remote workers are, almost by definition, highly-independent. And while many people thrive under this model, they can't do it alone. A handy electronic personal assistant (in the form of a to-do list app or written calendar) will pull you through your most hectic days intact. As it turns out, there are many different ways to forget to do something. Retrieval failure is when you know you have a task you need to get done but you simply can't for the life of you remember what it is. Then there's interference, where you mix up what you already did yesterday with what's to be done today. You can also simply have information go through one ear and out the other, failing to store it in your memory bank (an especially common problem when you're already busy or overworked).

How can you avoid these varied memory pitfalls? It's fairly simple, especially when it comes to work. Developing a strong habit of immediately putting assigned work into a task manager, along with due-date reminders. This prevents all of the above issues. You can check off recurring tasks to be sure they're actually completed every time. Indeed, hospitals are implementing more rigorous checklist protocols to improve surgical procedures and prevent patient fatalities around the world [2].

Organization also allows you the opportunity to plan out your day to maximize efficiency and minimize task-switching. This allows you to know exactly how much time you have to spend on a task and when to call in for reinforcements. On a weekly or monthly scale, you can balance your projects appropriately to avoid crunch times and major lulls.

Self-Confidence

If you're thinking of kissing the cubicle lifestyle behind, you're likely feeling a mix of emotions. Somewhere in there may very well be a healthy dose of self-doubt. To be an effective remote team member, you need to have the ability to communicate effectively and confidently with coworkers, managers and clients. You may find yourself (politely) fighting to head up projects you believe in or making the case for taking the company in a certain direction. Doing either from a distance can be tricky if you don't project conviction. A bit of faith in your ability to learn along the way couldn't hurt, either. Your own evaluation of your capabilities impacts how you tackle problems in a major way.

Problem-Solving

If you've ever had your internet go out at home when you're relaxing in front of the TV, imagine the stress of the loss of internet when you're in the middle of crunching numbers for an important work project. Remote workers often have backups for their backups in the event of an emergency. A local coffee shop can provide internet, your old laptop from seven years ago can open spreadsheets in crunch moments, and online dupes of popular programs can be used in the middle of a crisis.

As a remote employee, you may not have regular access to everyone on your team. This may cause problems to arise that you'll need to solve – solo. You need to understand when an issue requires outside help or if it's something you can handle on your own. It wastes everyone's time to play hot potato with a task. Flexibility is also a necessary skill for telecommuters. You may just end up adding many more tools to your toolbox than you originally imagined.

Whether you're just starting out as a remote worker, you've been doing it for years or you're still working toward that office-free life, picking up skills that will make your job easier and your resumé shinier is always a great idea.

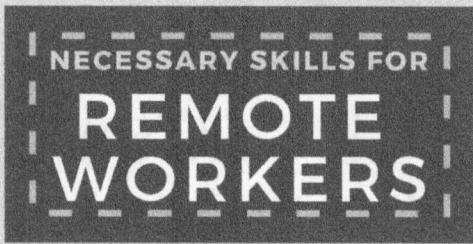

NECESSARY SKILLS FOR REMOTE WORKERS

SELF-MOTIVATION
Being self-motivated isn't simply a personality trait -- it's a muscle that you can develop and strengthen over time that will benefit remote workers

HUMILITY
With the self-directed nature of remote work, you're going to come face-to-face with the possibility of failure

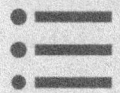

ORGANIZATION
A handy electronic personal assistant -- in the form of a to-do list app or written calendar -- will pull you through your most hectic day

SELF-CONFIDENCE
To be an effective remote team member, you need to have the ability to communicate effectively and confidently with coworkers, managers and clients

PROBLEM-SOLVING
Remote workers often have backups for their backups in the event of an emergency -- from internet to equipment to tools and more, you'll need to be ready

Chapter References

[1] Fishbach A (2018). How to Keep Working When You're Just Not Feeling It; *Harvard Business Review*.

[2] Thomassen O, Espeland A, Søfteland E, Lossius HM, Heltne JK & Brattebø G (2011). Implementation of checklists in health care; learning from high-reliability organisations; *Scand J Trauma Resusc Emerg Med.*, 19:53.

12

RESOURCES FOR REMOTE WORKERS

For remote workers, the toolbox is everything. We're not talking about the good old-fashioned hammer and nails here, either. The resources, applications, computer-based programs and other tools allow them to live a lifestyle away from the office. Randy Rayess over at Harvard Business Review [1] outlined the five necessary needs of a virtual workforce: convenience, transparency, accountability, communication and trust. Each of these factors benefit from having resources to appropriately support their place in the employer-employee relationship. As he points out, with over 3.3 million people working remotely, the need for effective and streamlined job tools is bigger than ever.

On the opposite end of the spectrum from appropriate resources is being overloaded with clunky, overlapping or inefficient tools. So many platforms claim to solve all friction issues in remote employment settings, but the truth is there's rarely a one-size-fits-all solution. Unless your company has built an internal system with everything you need and nothing you don't, you're likely going to be cobbling together your toolkit from a variety of sources. It's important to be selective, so your attention isn't spread too thin. For example, having six difference messaging apps for communication with coworkers will inevitably lead to an inefficient use of your time. It may take a bit of extra work, but migrating work conversations to a single channel allows you to avoid constantly switching context or allowing important tasks to slip through the cracks.

Let's run through some of the more common resources for remote employees below, keeping in mind you're unlikely to need each and every one.

Cloud Storage and Computing

Used correctly, cloud storage and computing are the perfect solution to some of the most pressing problems relating to convenience for remote workers. OneDrive, Dropbox, Google Drive and Box are some of the common big names you might recognize. If you're struggling to figure out which platform meets your needs, many comparisons have been made between these systems. Some are HIPPA-compliant, while others are more user-friendly. Some are generally used in specific fields and niches for their unique value propositions. But what benefits specifically do they offer?

Take Google Drive, for example. You can share documents, spreadsheets and other files with coworkers, managers and even people outside the company. The share settings allow you to avoid accidental overwrites to important documents, and having a single version of a file that's stored on the cloud means you don't have to keep track of multiple versions of the same item. This is especially important when telecommuting employees don't have the ability to speak face-to-face with others on their team about modifying documents.

Depending on the day-to-day functions of your role, these cloud computing systems may even obviate the need for other expensive tools.

Project Management

A web- or network-based project management tool like Asana or Trello allows for transparency throughout a team and even the company. Everyone is aware of who is responsible for which tasks, their progress on those tasks and how work is spread around a team. You can assign projects to people, set due-dates and generally ensure everyone is held accountable for their own pieces of the whole. That transparency and accountability will go far when it comes to trust both on the side of the remote worker and the company.

Each version of a task manager generally has a different interface style, making it difficult to easily switch between options. Make sure you carefully evaluate the options before selecting one for your company to avoid downtime as everyone learns the new system.

Communication

This is probably one of the most flooded areas of a remote

employee's toolkit. The ways to communicate are essentially endless in today's highly-connected world. In the US, the top messaging apps are Facebook Messenger, WhatsApp, SMS and iMessage. In fact, you likely have at least a few of these installed on your smartphone right now. For more secure communication, some use Signal for enhanced privacy. Work-specific messaging applications include Slack, whose tagline is *Where Work Happens*. On top of that, many products also allow for chats or messages inside their platforms. You can see how this can get overwhelming if telecommuters are expected to check each of these channels of communication regularly.

Email is generally simple, as most companies have settled into a specific provider such as Microsoft Outlook or G Suite. Phone calls often happen with a regular landline or cell phone number with remote workers, but to protect privacy and enhance the safety of employees, tools like Join.me and Zoom.us allow for web-based calls, video chats and screen-sharing. Shindig and Webex are similar, but they're more geared toward full, large-scale video conferencing with multiple members.

Personal Tasks Managers

Similar to a project manager, task managers help keep you accountable for your own to-do list. Apps like Todoist can be a totally private tool for remote workers to help manage their daily, weekly and monthly responsibilities. You can set recurring events, organize by project list, view your upcoming tasks and even see how productive you are over time.

Image and Document Editing

This is about as old as computers themselves, but if you're working remotely, you'll soon find just how important it is to choose which programs you use to open and edit documents, images and files. Apache OpenOffice is a great (and free) alternative to the traditional Microsoft Office suite, including programs for word documents, spreadsheets, presentations and more. Microsoft has been migrating over the past few years from a buy-once payment system to an ongoing subscription for the use of the basics like Word and Excel, making them an expensive option for some.

The issue is often two-fold in choosing less common tools, however. The first is the ability of other computers to read documents and the second is the learning curve for new programs. Both can be overcome, but you'll need to think about whether it's worth your time to struggle with these problems.

Timekeeping and Accounting

If you're working on a freelance or hourly contract job remotely, chances are good that you'll need an effective way to log your hours on projects. Platforms like Upwork come with this feature built into them, but for independently-managed work, you may need something like ClockIt. This again plays into accountability, transparency and trust between remote employees and their employers.

For remote freelancers, accounting software or a web-based resource like Wave are invaluable. It makes tax time infinitely easier, and you can easily see how your expenses stack up against your income.

If you're considering transitioning into remote work, it's important to understand the importance of the decisions you make when filling your toolbox. Depending on the costs involved, you may or may not be able to change things up later on down the road. For those who have already been telecommuting, the opportunity to trim the fat may save time, money and energy.

Chapter References

[1] Rayess R (2015). 5 Basic Needs of Virtual Workforces, *Harvard Business Review*.

13

RESOURCES FOR EMPLOYERS OF ASPIRING & CURRENT REMOTE WORKERS

When you think about the physical items and resources you need to fill a brick-and-mortar office, it's easy to imagine your employees' needs. Their days tend to look the same and their requirements are often straightforward. Desks and chairs, computers and printers, break areas and restrooms. When it comes to remote workers, however, the resources you provide to your remote workers as a business changes drastically. You likely have no idea what the inside of your telecommuting employees' homes look like. You may or may not have a crystal clear idea of how they structure their days. They might be working with technology you didn't choose or operating systems with which you're not familiar. However, if you want to build effective teams of remote workers, you can't just leave everything up to them.

There are too many tools to count out in the world right now, many of which perform identical or overlapping functions. This means that, left to their own devices, your telecommuting workforce is unlikely to select options by chance which work well together. If some employees prefer Slack for business communications while others use Google Hangouts, you're going to end up with too many people dropping the ball due to missed messages or wasted time spent regularly checking a wide range of platforms. To optimize your remote teams, it's time to think about streamlining the tools and resources everyone uses. If your remote workforce is experiencing issues, throwing technological fixes at a deeper problem probably isn't your best response. As Sean Graber pointed out over at Harvard Business Review [1], You may need to consider going back to the basics instead of piling more tools on top.

There will also be tools only you or people in managerial roles use. These outline big-picture trajectories for a department or company, help with behind-the-scenes issues and track performance metrics.

Company Policy Templates

If you're a larger company, chances are very good that you already have plenty of policies outlining expected employee behaviors in the office. However, what about the digital workplace? For those businesses that are considering expanding telecommuting options, it may be a good idea to pull together some new written company policies on expectations for your remote employees.

Communication which occurs when people aren't face-to-face can cause friction through a number of pitfalls. People's feelings may be hurt when humor or sarcasm are read instead of heard. Lunch breaks or available hours may not be respected by managers, accompanying an expectation that team members are always *on*. That can have knock-on effects for both employee well-being, as well as their productivity levels. If you work with private or sensitive data, you'll need to have firm rules around how that information can be accessed by off-site systems. There may even be issues related to how coworkers treat one another given the regular use of personal messaging apps.

Setting boundaries, guidelines and expectations in advance of hiring remote employees or shifting an in-office role into telecommuting allows you to move forward confidently as a company. Sites like Workable even offer templates for everything from attendance to dress codes for when employees meet with customers, partners or vendors.

Top-Down Task Management

Under most circumstances, as an employer, the last thing you want to do is be in the business of micromanaging the daily to-do list of your employees. The best candidate for a job is generally one who understands their role within the company and works independently to keep up with the small pieces required to form the whole project. That independence is part of what makes his or her position remote-capable. So while you can certainly have some suggestions regarding individual taskmasters and to-do list applications, your focus should instead be on tools which allow for a top-down view of projects.

Web- and app-based tools like Asana and Trello are good

examples of these. Managers can assign a larger goal with the intention of having team members fill in their own roles within the project. They can also set up templates for each person's expected role in a project and track completion over time. These apps also allow the whole team to see tasks which have been previously completed, as well as previous notes on them.

Calendars

Remote workers often benefit from the flexibility of their new schedules, but they may also need to be more careful than ever about updating team members about their availability. Google Calendar is popular for many organizations due to the ease of use and G Suite integration. You can assign new calendars by team member, projects, task type or any other metric you find useful. The beauty of digital calendars is their ability to toggle individual calendars on and off, allowing everyone to check for overlaps in schedules and projects. Meetings and busy times for individual employees can be easily noted. Vacation days and sick leave are simple to update. Regular tasks can be repeated. With shared calendars, you can outline the longer-term trajectory of larger or complex goals, as well.

Human Resources

For larger companies, a human resources employee/department is again something you'll almost certainly already have and which just needs to be adapted for the specific challenges of remote employment. Smaller businesses, however, may just be starting to experience the growing pains which happen without HR there to grease the cogs. If you're still before the point in time where it makes sense to hire an internal human resources person, there are plenty of options to outsource this service. These companies can take on a surprising number of tasks, from payroll to benefit-plan management, and even recruiting new employees. They're often the tool you didn't think you needed –until you do. It's nearly impossible to avoid issues between employees over years together in business as you integrate new people and let go of others. Depending on what sector your business is in, there are also safety concerns HR can help with, including assistance-tracking actual hours worked by remote employees to hold them accountable. If your business deals with any sensitive information, HR can provide training and protocols and even offer follow-up efficacy tests for compliance.

It can feel daunting to take the plunge with such a huge change in your business's structure, but there are plenty of resources out there aimed specifically at making remote work viable for companies. If you've struggled with this decision, it may be good to start experimenting with part-time telecommuting options and test the waters using a bare-bones toolkit. With some proven successes under your belt, the transition will become important for employees and employers alike.

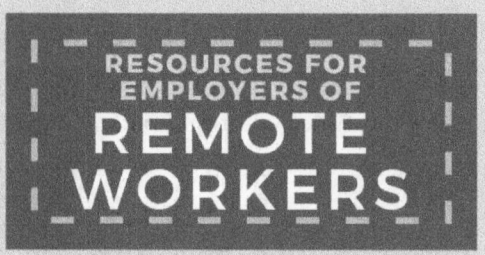

RESOURCES FOR EMPLOYERS OF REMOTE WORKERS

COMPANY POLICY TEMPLATES

For those businesses that are considering expanding the option for telecommuting, it's smart to pull together some new written company policies on expectations for your employees

TOP-DOWN TASK MANAGEMENT

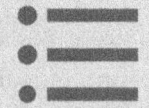

With task managers, employers can assign a larger goal with the intention of having team members fill in their own roles within the project, checking progress along the way

CALENDARS

The beauty of digital calendars -- like Google Calendar -- is their ability to toggle individual calendars on and off, allowing everyone to check for overlaps in schedules and projects as well as meetings

HUMAN RESOURCES

Human resources contract companies can take on a surprising number of tasks, from payroll to benefit plan management and even recruiting new employees

Chapter References

[1] Graber S (2015). Why Remote Work Thrives in Some Companies and Fails in Others, *Harvard Business Review*.

14

FUTURE DIRECTIONS FOR REMOTE WORK

Most of the recent research on remote work indicates that it's not going away any time soon. A Gallup poll [1] from just a few years ago indicated that more Americans than ever are working remotely. Those who split time between home offices and corporate buildings are spending more time in the former as well. On top of that, many people are reporting new access to work-from-home options that hadn't existed previously. Certain industries, such as transportation, computer and information systems and mathematical fields, are more than ready to embrace the shift to telecommuting. Others, like the sciences, engineering and education, are still either unable or unwilling to make the switch. And while remote work isn't the solution for every workplace woe, its growing popularity among bother employers and job seekers makes it important to understand.

What are some of the top predictions for remote work in the near and far future? To answer those questions, we'll need to go over what goes into making those guesses. A few months back, Virgin Galactic founder Richard Branson spoke about how he sees the future of the workforce moving away from the standard nine to five. While part of this is based on an idealized future that assumes basic tasks are automated, he also discusses his belief in blurring the boundaries of "work and play." Some may rejoice at a future where they're not limited to set weekend hours, while others might view these changes as contributing to an "always on" culture. Either way, he's probably not wrong. Employment opportunities are opening up in sectors of the workforce that only require a laptop and an internet connection. More and more people are forging ahead with new companies and contract work that allows them to work from anywhere. There are still plenty of unknowns in play, such as how local and national policies will support or undermine efforts to move toward remote work employment. There are, however, quite a few well-informed suppositions to be made.

Going Green

With increased scrutiny of carbon emissions in every sphere of life, companies are constantly looking for ways to cut down on their environmental footprint. Many have already started making a dent with LEED certified buildings and changes in product packaging. Moving people from point A (home) to B (work) in the most inefficient way possible (single-user vehicles) is a waste that can't be ignored much longer. Remote work has the opportunity to drastically reduce the use of fossil fuels in both the short and longer term. Pilot programs in the early 2000s found that you could reduce pollution by 25-tons each year when only 4,500 telecommuters worked from home an average of 1.8 days a week. Knock on effects include families investing in only one car instead of two to support a regular American lifestyle.

Improved Tools

Whether your coworkers are two or 2,000 miles away, there will always be a need for effective tools for communication. Between video conferencing, messaging applications and cloud information platforms, there are plenty of advancements that can still be made in the coming years. For those who see the integration of work into home life as a dangerous trend, some of these tools also come with enhanced privacy settings. For example, we're starting to see programs that turn off notifications after work hours. You can also get many with straightforward vacation settings, such as customizable away messages.

Gmail's introduction of the autofill email responses is now helping people hit Inbox Zero faster. Beyond video conferences, you could even start seeing advancements in virtual reality for an immersive experience. To touch again upon the green factor, imagine the perks to the planet if your board of directors didn't have to fly from around the country or the world for a weekend.

Integration of Remote Workers

As remote work becomes more commonplace, you're going

to start seeing the integration of the tools telecommuters use everywhere within companies. Since there are no other options for communication – such as face to face interactions – remote workers may just be the first to master tools. That mastery can benefit the rest of the company in a variety of ways, starting with the effective use of those tools by everyone throughout the business. The role of telecommuters within an institution will come into question less and less as the idea of working remotely becomes more commonplace. They will be seen as less of an inconvenience and as a regular part of the team.

Increased Use of Specific Skills

For companies that have made their mark on the world by being behemoths in their industry, they may soon find that the sleek, flexible and multi-talented remote worker is exactly what they need to stay relevant. With social media platforms like Twitter, Instagram, Facebook and Snapchat cutting down the lifecycle of any new marketing idea or product, effective strategies for businesses will play off of the exact strengths you'd find in your average remote worker. They're often well-versed in figuring out new systems on the fly, they can pivot their work quickly to respond to changes from the top-down or bottom-up, and they're independent enough to require little oversight.

Happier Workers

In most recent measures of employment satisfaction, remote

workers tend to come out on top. They're happier in their jobs, and while they may struggle with certain aspects like fitting into the larger work culture, they enjoy the flexibility they're given. Parents are able to be present for more of their children's' lives. Those with physical or mental disabilities can more easily maintain jobs that work well within their limitations. They're spending less money and time on transportation. They're not surrounding themselves with people they don't particularly like on a daily basis. Plus, they're often more able to take vacations or work from environments that make them happy.

The future for remote work in America is both bright and complex. While there are plenty of factors that can and likely will affect the trajectory of this new employment model, its popularity is definitely on an upswing. Between personal benefits for workers and professional benefits for employers, it's certainly not going away any time soon. The support systems for telecommuting are growing in many industries. There have been a few setbacks as specific companies, such as Yahoo, scale back in their remote work programs, but these appear to be outliers as opposed to the norm. With the lives and livelihoods of millions of Americans in the balance, the future of remote work is more important than ever.

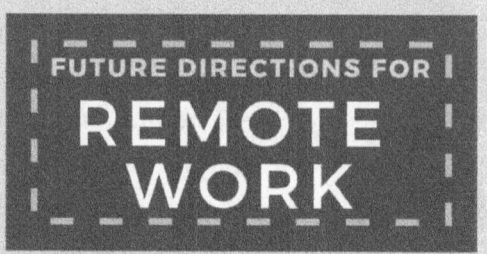

FUTURE DIRECTIONS FOR REMOTE WORK

GOING GREEN

Remote work has the opportunity to drastically reduce the use of fossil fuels in both the short and long term

IMPROVED TOOLS

Between video conferencing, messaging apps and cloud information platforms, there's plenty of room for advancements

INTEGRATION OF REMOTE WORKERS

The role of remote workers in a company will come into question less as the idea of working remotely becomes more commonplace

INCREASED USE OF SPECIFIC SKILLS

Future effective strategies for businesses will play off of the exact strengths you'd find in your average remote worker

HAPPIER WORKERS

In most recent measures of employment satisfaction, remote workers tend to come out on top — a trend that will likely continue

Chapter References

[1] Clifton, J. *State of the American Workplace: Employee Engagement Insights for U.S. Business Leaders* (2017); Gallup.

www.ingramcontent.com/pod-product-compliance
Lightning Source LLC
Chambersburg PA
CBHW070655220526
45466CB00001B/452